waterways poetry

Catching the Cascade

Big Wishes from [signature]

This book has come to you from Bardaid

Rrrantr 5th b'day Nov 14.

waterways.

releasing new voices, revealing new perspectives

Catching the Cascade

the waterways series, 2009
a contemporary poetry series of flipped eye publishing

First Edition
Copyright © Paul Lyalls, 2009
Cover Image found in a skip
Cover Design © Petraski, flipped eye publishing, 2009

ISBN-13: 978-1-905233-28-1

Some of the poems in Catching the Cascade have appeared in *Gargoyle Magazine*, *The London Magazine*, *Trespass*, *The Main Street Journal*, *Rising*, Penguin's *Michael Rosen's A-Z of Children's Poetry* and *My Hackney, my Hackney*.

Editorial work for this book was supported by the Arts Council of England.

The text is typeset in Lacuna, a font created by Glashaus Design, and Palatino from Linotype GmbH.

Printed and Bound in the United Kingdom

LOTTERY FUNDED

For Joan, Cordelia, Honor and Suria

Catching the Cascade

Paul Lyalls
2009

Special thanx throughout the years go to – everyone who shone at Express Excess, especially John Bush, Gretchen Laddish, Markus Birdman esq, Apples and Snakes (past and present), the Roundhouse, Pleasance Theatre, the Poetry Society, The Barbican education team, the Arts Council, Make Believe Arts crew, Dana C, Donald Dee & Poetry and Poppadums, Mark Gwynne Jones 'n' Francesca Beard, Charlie and the Goole Gate-Junction theatre, All Change, The BBC, The Enterprise team – especially Scott, Jim and Michael, Tim Turnbull, Ruth and the Holloway festival, all at St Aidans, Paul and 57 Productions, Ann 'n' Bri, Rommy, Luis and Tamara, John Hegley, Michael Rosen, Jan Woolf, the squad players of Tuesday Knights, The Brent Library team, Richard Tyrone Jones, Karl 'The Lens' Dolenc, Peter B Darwin, all the gigs, shows, festivals and schools I've enjoyed working and performing with, and flipped eye —Nii, Jacob and the wonderful Niall O'Sullivan.

Paul Lyalls, London

Catching the Cascade

THE VALUE OF WALES

Its chief contribution to the UK
must be as a unit of measurement,
as night after night
a news desk declares,
"An area of rainforest,
the size of Wales disappears every year"
or, "The amount of water
London loses through its creaking Victorian pipes
would fill a swimming pool
the size of Wales."
Every part of the world has a similar unit of measurement:
in the United States it's an area the size of New Jersey;
on mainland Europe the reference, more often than not,
is Slovenia—which appropriately happens to be
98.4 percent *the size of Wales.*
But just how accurate is Wales
as a unit of measurement?
Just how constant is that land mass?
It's worth remembering that at low tide
Wales measures 20,761 SQ KM
whereas at high tide it's only 20,449 SQ KM—
and to really put it into context,
each year coastal erosion erodes an area of Wales
the size of Central Swansea.
For those of you in Europe trying to visualise this,
that's the equivalent of an area the size
of downtown Ljubljana.

TIME

Our hotelier pointed out that
all the clocks in all the hotel rooms
told different times.
So, in some rooms you were late
and in other rooms you were early.
"It's not a problem," said the Nuclear Physicist
breakfasting on the next table,
"Time actually happens four times slower
than we think."
"Not round here it doesn't!" rejoined our hotelier,
"Round here, time happens really fast!"
At which I gazed out of the window
and surveyed the lifeless two-street
regional-coastal town—
which had about as much going
on as a letter that never arrives.
If ever there was an argument
for there not being a God,
this place was it.
"In fact," continued our hotelier, "you can tell
how much is going on around here
by the all the things that are happening:
in September there's a Wicker Doll fair,
in October a Poetry Festival *and* a Science Convention,
in November there's Bonfire Night
and before you know it,
it's Christmas.
Right, who's got time for another cup of tea?"

THE ANATOMY OF A BOOKSHOP

English Literature
was beside the drinking fountain.

American Literature
was over near the vending machine.

Romance
next to the fire escape.

Philosophy
was between the first and second floors.

Crime
could be found next to the tills.

Politics
was below ethics.

Self-Help
by the mirror.

Making the World a Better Place
was next to books on children's names.

Religion
was next to Fantasy.

Poetry
was down in the basement
with Wines, Beers and Spirits.

HARD, FAST AND BEAUTIFUL

In John Ford's Stagecoach (1939)
(which raised the Western genre
to artistic status),
she was the 'Saloon Girl' Dallas
who had been forced out of town
by puritanical women.
When 'The Ringo Kid' (John Wayne)
proposes to her, she says —
But you don't know me,
you don't know who I am.
I know all I want to know,
he says.
Seeing a glimmer of hope
she asks the drunken doctor
(Thomas Mitchell) —
Is that wrong for a girl like me?
If a man and a woman
love each other,
it's all right,
ain't it Doc?

ONLY IN THE MOVIES

Some things only happen in the movies
as only the movies can depict.
Any lock
can be picked with a credit card
or a paper clip.
Cars explode when struck by a single bullet.
All rednecks wear dungarees
and have a mullet.
You will easily survive
any battle or war zone
unless you make the fatal mistake
of showing someone a picture
of your sweetheart back home.
The movies make the Far East easy for us to understand:
evil Arabs speak in Arabic
the good ones speak *A-me-ri-can*.
A single match will light up
a room the size of St Paul's Cathedral.
The person you least suspect
always turns out to be the most evil.
In car chases it's always the police car that crashes
and any woman becomes beautiful and debonair
by simply taking off her glasses and letting down her hair.
All bombs are fitted with big red digital timers
that show you exactly when they are about to blow
and all bombs can only be defused
with three seconds left to go.
From any Parisian window
the Eiffel Tower is always in view
and for some reason ninja warriors
will only attack one at a time—

sometimes they even go as far as to form an orderly queue.
And finally, concerning the police,
two things that are always true:
cases can only be solved
by detectives who have been suspended,
and no crime can be solved
unless a strip club has been attended.

GOD'S COFFEE

Gazing into my cappuccino
I saw that the face of Christ
had appeared on the top,
formed in the sprinkles and the froth.
I told everyone else in the café
because I thought they should know.
Most agreed
but quite a few thought
it actually looked more like Russell Crowe.
One sad soul,
who was clearly living in The Twilight Zone,
thought it bore more of a resemblance
to Catherine Zeta Jones—
but to me it was the face of Christ
as he must have looked,
as he gazed down from the cross
lost in a heavenly requiem.
So, I added some chocolate sprinkles
to see if it would reveal
the Nativity scene of old Bethlehem
but I had to make do with the Batman emblem.

THE LABEL'S PRAYER

Versace,
which art in Harrods,
hallowed be thy label.
Thy King's Road come,
Yves Saint Lauren,
as it can be seen in Cosmopolitan,
touched down High Street South Kensington
and, to a lesser extent, Hoxton.
Give us this day our daily *cred*
and forgive us our overdraft excesses
as we forgive those
who refuse a refund
because 'within 30 days' passes.
And lead us not into TK Max or River Island,
and deliver us from Diesel
for thine is the Calvin Klein,
the Prada and the Gucci.
For Dolce and Gabbana,
Armani.

THE FLOOR LENGTH 1927 CRISTERO REBELLION

Images of an uprising on a bullet-studded dress,
a study in ammunition and its cause and effect,
cut to ribbons, cut to beauty—Miss Universe no less.
Miss Mexico calling, revolutionaries falling
—apart from those shown hanging by the roadside
—now we're talking accessorize.
The bloodied face of God,
the rifles of the firing squad.
Should a skirt depict
violent social conflict?
The Cristero uprising
is something Mexico wants left forgotten
but sweet Rosa Maria
swirled a shapely reminder
around her legs and her bottom.
Should fashion depict armed retribution?
Is there a solution?
Just give us a twirl love
not a bloody revolution.

FULLA

The first doll with Muslim values,
has kicked Barbie off the number one spot
—at least in the Arab world.
There are other Muslim dolls
but Fulla is the leader of the pack.
She doesn't have Barbie's lifestyle,
no flashy accessories, endless outfits,
just a Hijab and a prayer mat.
More importantly, she has dark eyes.
Her makers claim
this isn't just another Barbie doll.
Fulla is honest, loving and caring
and she respects her mother and father.
Just wait till she becomes a teenager.

QUIFF

If you can gel your hair
into a duck's arse
when everyone else
has a Manchester fringe;
If you have hair that stands on end
when all around you
are bad-hair-day winds;
If you have a spiky buzz-cut
when all else is bobbed and trimmed;
If some white van driver
drops the window and yells out "Billy Idol!"
—when all around are sporting
a silly Vidal…
Sassoon;
If you can walk into the barber's shop
with an Elvis Presley record sleeve
and say to the man with the scissors
"This is what I need";
If you can wake up in a morning,
and your hedge is still up there performing;
If, when the Oasis look was all,
you remained true to your Wonder Wall.
If you refuse to answer the fashion call
by letting your hair fall,
then…and only then…
there is no *If*.
You, my son,
have a quiff!

LEAVE YOUR MESSAGE AFTER THE BEAT (PERFORMANCE POETRY IS...)

Bristling with insight, milking every sense of meaning,
it's a fly on the wall study of a fly on the wall,
an aria of decadent route one lyricism
spun by frontier pushing pens,
words to the real, socio-flow
brought to you direct by Lord and Lady Biro.
Alive with detail from
an 'off each and all four walls' little known world,
sharp and fragmented as a broken mirror,
rolling with reflection
and self-fascinated self-exploration.
With an 'on the house' cocktail
of breathtaking confessional meets in-depth suspect,
that's 'checking in from downtown',
featuring the sharpest of the sharp,
with sparks flying off of them in a language lit dark.
Be of the poem, but not in the poem.
Featuring writers who never appeared in their
own reviews,
smeared with cool outsider status
weaving urban mantras to save us —
The King of Spin....The Queen of In-between
......The Merchant of Menace!
Half real, half dream, with a heart that beats
like a paddle steamer on a mercy mission —
it's not in the spirit of appreciative enquiry though,
it's a lifestyle choice
and the world's greatest journeys are the
words that give them voice.
If the devil has all the best tunes,
the angels all the best hymns,
then somewhere in-between are
poets giving words wings.

BLOODY POETRY

A poet has as much purpose in life as balls on a priest.
Poets are lost, they have nowhere to go—
like a fly without a window—
but still they linger
like sliced bread in an unplugged toaster.
Poets explain the world, but they are not philosophers:
poets are married to language,
from this many beautiful poems are born,
philosophers sleep around with ideas,
the names of which they cannot remember
come the dawn.
Poets have about as much chance
as a man nailing jelly to the ceiling.
Poets are few, poets are just stereotypes
with attitude.
They are on the crest of a ripple,
they need to say their lines like a new born baby
needs its mother nipple—
like a coyote, howling poetry.
Poets put the *petal* to the metal,
their lines hit you like a ram raid—
the running athlete of language,
toned supple and forceful,
the ballet of the word stage.
Its every movement harnesses
the power of the word,
generating reality feedback—
when I hear a poem
I hear life's kicking soundtrack.

BYRONIC SOUL

I'm a tortured poet.
I live in a tortured bedsit,
cook with a tortured frying pan.
I go out with a tortured girl,
live in a very tortured world,
a tortured poet's got a tortured soul.
I take my clothes to a tortured launderette,
I perform shows that are full of pain and regret,
nightly I hit tortured lows,
it's about as tortured as it can get.
I read tortured books,
possess a wide range of tortured looks,
I have a tortured future, tortured flashbacks,
tortured kids, tortured bicycle clips,
tortured chips on my tortured shoulders.
I get more tortured as I get older.
Right from the start
I pour out my heart
that's been torn apart
wider than a canyon.
It's been broken more times than
the world ten thousand metre record
has been broken by a Kenyan.
I wandered lonely as a traffic warden,
feel these tortured feelings,
I've seen the best minds of my generation
destroyed at bad poetry readings.
Yeah, I'm tortured, I really burn,
I've suffered for my art
and now it's your turn.

I LOVE YOU I LOVE YOU

Where were you when Kurt Cobain died,
the night he tried out for that big band in the sky
—the one that can't make music
because guitars don't enter heaven?
There's a silence from above that proves this.
I wonder if his little girl cried? Did she know him?
Would she have let him choose it?
This guy, to whom the rock writers
pay all their high respect without a single mention
of his daughter neglect, is now unable to direct
any love towards her.
Left half alone Francis cannot be daddy's little girl
and mixing kids with rock 'n' roll
is a corrosive cocktail that changes colours like a bleach.
Not quite a pacific north-west orphan,
she still has *Love* in her world,
but of you she has none
and weren't you the guy that swore,
No, I don't have a gun?
Binding words and chords
and thrashing guitars into something
beautiful and hard—yes, you really starred—
but the real marks that carve
are the ones that are left on her:
she, that is denied all the love
you could have offered if you'd
only survived.
Still, now it's done and there's
no rewind and as for Francis, well,
nevermind.

AWAKE TO A KISS

Once upon a time,
in the beginning of my mind,
fair princesses more lovely than the dawn
roamed the earth with tough-on-tangle hair
or were awakened from their dreaming
by princes with boy-band looks
who would declare
"Your garden has got quite
out of hand and your stepmother is difficult
and bewildering—
between you and me
I think she eats children,
on all fours, even yours."
Charmed by these words
and the way they were spoken,
grateful that the evil magic was broken,
she fell madly in love, as one does.
"My heart is yours, please unlock it!
Are you pleased to see me fair prince,
Or is that a glass coffin in your pocket?"
Now princes may be handsome and kind
but they only have marriage and child-bearing on their mind;
while the only thing about a princess's appearance that's wrong
is that it's all she's judged on.
So, as you are happy, so be wise,
fairy tales are reality in disguise,
and this you'll find
is exactly as it happened,
except it didn't rhyme.

THE LOVE OF THE BARMAID

She is the captive female
that must walk or stand,
depending upon the demand,
within her enclosed space.
Allowing those that gaze
or flick a look
the unasked right to study and learn
her features, form and face.
They take delight as they do so,
for she to them represents
the submitting woman whose company
need not be earned or understood.
All it takes is just a word or a sound
or a movement unheard and she'll be
drawn over as if contract bound.
Always quick to attend
and slow to disagree,
not able to escape or argue too far,
not able to be really real,
not able to be free—
looked at, looked upon, looked lovely
in varying degrees;
to many men she is the answer,
she's a '*same again*' fantasy.

THE CULT OF RELATIONSHIPS

The truth is like a sleeping viper, don't poke it.
The truth is men and women are different,
but try not to live with or without it.
Nothing is eternal, love has its span,
sex lasts as long as it can.
Even gigantic tubs of margarine run out eventually,
but hell, it made some great toast if you see what I mean...
Ignore the romantic lies, relationships one-size, fit some.
Metrify and simplify, if you have to have flaws
then make 'em attractive—
when it goes beyond optimism it'll work.
One day all this will be lost like tears in a power shower
so find out what kind of coal gets your train going into that station
and fill up your bath with it to overflowing.
Take a walk across that mystical bridge of connection,
throw a coin into the sexual jukebox,
make your personal selection
and let your love making
crackle like a wild west gun fight
into the night.
So what if men are from Middlesborough
and women are from Harvey Nicks?
Use your imagination
or try a once in a while conversation
that's a scorching sight for the mind's eye.
Make your love making clearer
and then you just might prevent your relationship
from turning into a piece of fringe theatre.
Like a 3D fairy tale, take it higher,
put your hand in the flames and you'll
soon understand the nature of the fire.

LET'S (YOU'RE THE GAL FOR MY CORRAL)

Let's call it love,
call it infatuation,
call it logic evaporation.
Let's call it seeing chick flicks,
car-chase cold turkey.
Let's call it saying
"Baby, you've done so much for me lately."
Out of this world,
as perfect and individual as pearls,
like a star about to explode.
Out of all the girls from around the globe
you're the one who makes my heart-light strobe.
Call it that feeling of awe,
of having too much
but still wanting more.
Let's call it love when you get
that feeling there ain't no beating,
the sensation you get when you
mix shopping with eating.
Let's call it love when she
reduces your best line to a stammer:
"Oh b-b-baby, you put the amour in glamour."
Let's call it love when, irrespective of the day and time,
she's looking like a serious down payment
on a diamond mine.
Let's call it love when you use
extravagant language and all it conveys
to describe how
her sparkling spirit sashays
through the shadows of your soul

and her touch turns the base metals
of your being into shimmering gold.
Let's call it love when her eyes, lips
and thoughts burn you down below.
When you feel something so intense
you can't even tell it to your pillow.

ASK THE AUDIENCE? PHONE A FRIEND? GO FIFTY-FIFTY OR LISTEN TO YOUR HEART?

…and then she asks
the Holy Grail of all female questions:
"What are you thinking?"
And I think, what am I thinking?
I'm thinking, why did you have to ask that?
More importantly, I'm thinking
what *should* I be thinking?
I'm thinking that I should have thought about you more—
I'm thinking that
if we had our time again,
there's a thousand things I'd do differently—
but what I'm *really* thinking is
that the next time we go to IKEA
wouldn't it be great
if I were to get inside one of the display wardrobes,
stay silent, hide and wait…
until someone opens the doors,
then leap out
demanding to know,
"What country is this?"
But I know that at this moment
I shouldn't be thinking this.
So instead I say, "I'm thinking
that if a thousand years
is just a blink in time
then maybe we can gaze into each other's eyes forever."
And she says, "Wow, were you thinking that?"
And I say, "Kind of."
Then she kisses me, smiles, gazes into my eyes
and says, "Let's go to IKEA."

THROWING STONES

In gardens, up and down the land
they can be seen.
Each year, more and more appear,
larger than before,
looming over fences, distinct and clear.
Uglier than ever,
anything they meet is torn asunder,
the plastic garden furniture is no more.
Even the invincible brick barbecue meets its match,
the fishing gnomes have long since been dispatched,
the clothes line was terminally snapped.
Such ferocity, from such gentle sounding creations
with names like
Valley of Eden, The Panorama, Quest for Tomorrow and
Vale of Splendour...
They have even made the patio and lawn their own.
Behold, reaching out from one in ten suburban homes:
the conservatory!
It's not only put value on our house,
it's given value to our life.
Gaze in as we take afternoon tea
in little china cups,
gasp in awe as we slice the cake
bought from Marks and Spencer,
generous slices, enough for all.
I will stand and gaze through
its kaleidoscopic glass,
vent its blinds,
I will sit in my fortress of solitude,
think my thoughts,

wonder how we ever lived without one.
Throw frosty looks into the living room,
shocked that it could even be called that,
stunned that we ever spent meaningful time
in that hell hole.
At night we will lie awake marveling
at all it has bequeathed us.
Home ownership and interior design to live for
and the conservatory to dream of.

DOMINOS PIZZA – THE DREAM AND THE REALITY

We travel the world
discovering the best ingredients,
combinations of flavours
fusing Mexico and Japan into one.
We've got the pizza to suit your lifestyle,
take a fresh look…
our pizza embodies all that is natural in society —
instant sharing, maximum disposability.
We've got the slices to suit your mood swings,
combinations of image that reveal your potential.
We bring all of this to your door
in thirty minutes, maybe less, never more.
We are happy to meet your needs,
take your order,
fulfil your thin base, deep crust desires.
Nothing can come between us…

…whispering in the background.
Is there more than one of you?

We operate with smart hustle,
surf positive energy to succeed for you…

…the caller has an extremely young sounding voice…
Are you a child operating at random?

We are people on a mission,
investing our time, talent and unique energies….

...the sound of passing cars means you are in a call box.
That place is no homestead!

We are a team united around the world.
We will accomplish our duty...

...you hesitate about giving key information
like street names and numbers.

We are fanatical about our product.
We exist to offer it up for your satisfaction...

...there is loud music in the background. Many voices are
screaming and swearing– a party is going on.
Who will pay for your 8 slices of utopia?

Our vision is of exceptional people on a mission
with great personalities.
When you eat our pizza,
you consume not only the dream
but also a little of the maker—the architect of its design.
And you, you who have called upon us,
you are made up of that common human feeling
—that you are hungry and lazy and nothing in this world
will make you move off your arse.
So you called us.
Our pizza is made for you
and we were made for each other.

PROGRESS IN PROGRESS

There are no horizons in a city,
only those within yourself.
I couldn't tell where the city ended
and the people began,
there were only individuals
with crowd-like tendencies
and eternal hopefuls
dreaming of big fat redundancies.
I went through every street in the city
and couldn't find one person whom I remotely liked.
The revolving doors of human happiness
where jammed shut with people
pushing in every direction
apart from the right one.
To escape the city, I took to the country
...only to find that the city had got there first,
flanked on all sides by *ivory tower blocks.*
I felt like driving my fist into an oncoming truck
or smashing up a train
or injecting raw words straight into a vein.
I switch on the TV—which tells me,
apparently,
everything is
drifting towards a state of perfection
but never quite getting there.
Modern living is getting faster
and there are more twists in it than novelty pasta.
We prefer a little truth and a little lie
to a bigger, more factual picture
and life and death
take on different aspects

depending upon
which side of the street they're viewed from.
Inscribe the child with the tribe
or welcome to evolution MTV style—
and all the while
the cure for a lack of love remains
a long time coming.
We need another inept leader,
kerb-crawler or crank caller,
like a fish needs a trawler.
We have nothing to fear but soaring prices,
global warming, mass unemployment,
economic collapse, government by the
Liberal Democrats
and fear itself.
We are eating a starter in the
This-Wasn't-in-the-Brochure Diner.
A Fawlty Towers style waiter
will bring the main course later.

We all awake
in the same position,
a state of limited edition.
Morning re-arranging,
traffic lights changing
—*halt, who goes there?*
Giving freely the extras
keep the necessities bare.
The world revealed by a back-light,
dawn comes in the form of a song,
those who know the words sing along.
Adjust the setting,
gambling not betting.
Picture your face—only younger,
it's hard to picture it older.
Picture the faces of your past,
remember the force of childhood;
how did it get from there to here,
how long does anything last?
Turn left or right,
walk towards day-break or twilight.
Another door…
now can't be like before.
Gaze away into the day
or work, rest and play.
Worry yourself away
in a sea of panic,
re-arranging the deck chairs
on the Titanic.

PROVINCIAL REACTION

Northern Realism seized me by the collar.
It swung me around the dance floor
on a small town Saturday night.
I turned like a lathe, I swore,
I ached for Sunday morning
and the loneliness of shops never opening.
Thus caught in a life of process,
flux and change,
there is no clearly defined finishing line,
just a procession of illuminating moments.
Are we filled with an imaginary living
that bears no relation to how it's meant to be,
apart from the split moments of hesitation
when we are who we are?
Or do we suffer from a kind of honesty deprivation
that dulls reality?
They say there is as much beauty in a mile
as a thousand,
take your foot off the pedal,
there is no winner or gold medal.

OUT OF SIGHT OUT OF MIND

–to be read in the voice of Bob Dylan

You're gonna miss me when I'm gone…
until then sing along.
Words lethal as a spike,
a cynical slipperiness that's speared on sight.
Don't think twice, don't think again,
the times are a changing
but so are Chameleons.
Coruscating rhymes, freewheeling ideas,
from time to time everybody should look
in their rear view mirrors.
Anyone who lives in a house of cards
should make sure they don't slam their front door
too hard.
If you've looked all about and still feel you're without,
don't worry, don't inwardly scream and shout,
it's not important to be in Who's Who,
it's better that you're in you.
Lightening strikes, we've all got scorch marks
'cos happiness and loneliness are different seats
but it's the same ball park.
We've all got a challenge, that's what life is for,
Dylan took on the Beatles and Elvis,
maybe he didn't win, but he got a creditable draw.
We all know how bad living feels and how it's gone too soon,
so let's sing about it out of tune,
in a pitch that shrills
accompanied by a guitar that states—
This Machine Kills.

Dedicated to Mark Gwynne Jones, the Dylan of the East Midlands.

WRITERS ON THE STORM

Into the engine room of a Saturday night.
A spin cycle of light, noise inhalation,
overcrowded expectant fashion.
Body-wrecking, dream-spilling,
life-bending moments,
a slaughter of library books.
All knowledge is just agreement,
it's better to be lucky than smart,
it's all just a postcard from nowhere,
God exists and lives in a sugar cube—
 "Watch it mate you're spilling my life!"
On this night, a cup of coffee
gets more sleep then your average Josephine.
My drop dead gorgeous launderette,
she beckoned with come to the supermarket eyes
and said:
"I want to be loved in a way that I don't understand!"
Saturday night is a dog with two tails,
whilst hangover land is a scary faraway place
and the taste of fame
just got tastier.
Saturday night is between
thought and expression.
Saturday night is being caught in possession
of a good feeling.
Saturday night is a weapon.
Saturday night is being so drunk
you don't know where the ground is.

Rave new world
in a silver dress
mugging peoples sub-consciousness.
I'm not tired, I'm hysterical,
I know what the words mean
but I haven't got a clue what you're saying.
Saturday night has them dancing in the gallows,
buzzing like an electricity sub station.
If you can't be kind
at least be vague.
Saturday night is
a long night's journey into night
and we are as much influenced by the people
that we've met
as by the people that we never met.
Saturday night is Saturday night.
The day after is a derelict day
and the ocean's in motion all the time.
The way ahead was clear,
but it was the wrong road.

KISS THE BADGE

Kiss the badge,
you've got to kiss the badge
like you're on a first date
and it's late,
hold it tight
and all it stands for.
Caress the badge,
this moment right now
may never last,
under the blaze of the floodlight
let your lips go,
press them to the fabric of all it stands for.
This is the second you want all the world to know.
French kiss the badge
even though you've just met,
don't know each other's last names yet,
even though there are forty-thousand people watching,
put on a public display of affection.
Kiss the badge,
show it you care,
it's not about the money,
it's about pressing your lips
to the symbol of allegiance.
Romance the badge,
beauty is in the eye
of the three year contract holder,
with get out clauses
in case things go wrong–
or a bigger club comes along–
you can be gone
to a new badge to kiss.

It's not about avarice and greed,
being a role model or nine-month sentences,
it's about kissing without pretences.
Kiss the badge–this time it's going to be forever,
until the end of time
…injury time
and even *extra* time.
Kiss the badge, go all the way,
kiss it in the replay.

GOALS ARE HEAVEN SENT

Goodbye working week, the dream has begun,
goals bring fire to a 3pm journey's end,
a shimmy, a swaying of hips,
the steel stand sways, the movement twists.
The ball is precious, the feet come and go,
Feet leave no footprints when playing in snow.
Feet turn on a coin,
turn on a crowd,
turn the watching world upside down.
Goals are heaven sent—half chances are easy,
quarter chances astound,
scored only by those who wear
the natural born strikers crown.
The missing of an open goal becomes
the sticker-book gap of the footballers soul,
burying the rebound, but the ball wanders past the post
like Lazarus, or some other dead man from the Bible,
going for a stroll.
An unrippled net, a silenced ground, one to forget,
no goals this week– goals are heaven sent .
Saturday comes, the nine-to-five goes, the football flows,
the dream can begin,
if you don't score you cannot win.
'Goals are heaven sent' is the message carried in the
home crowd's reverberating roar,
as they demand an equaliser
even though the opposition have yet to score.
A voice with intent that's unable to relent,
whilst the field flows to dancing toes,

shimmying hips, passing gifts,
football that is total.
The dream can begin—the steel stands sway,
if you don't score you cannot win,
in football goals are everything.

EVERYONE IS A POET

Everyone is a poet:
everyone has said
something that strips away
a piece of the thin layer
that decorates life
or made a statement that nets
a leaping moment of being.
Let us take a walk over the bridge
of the difficult miracle
to where we can view anything as it really is,
even at the factory above the din of machinery
and the agony of changing metal,
something else became magical.
The lathe turner said it—
Don't you see? Everyone is a poet.

FAT CHANCE

Some of us are in the gutter
others are gawping at the stars
and then there are those of us
fixing cars.

DON'T TRY THIS AT HOME

Start the beamer,
thrash the beamer,
smash it into the housing estate.
Wave to the helicopter,
I ain't sick and I don't need a head doctor.
It ain't stealing when I take your car,
it's just another form of drug with which
you're not used to dealing.
My drug has more than highs and lows,
it's got 4-wheel drive accelerator feeling,
I thrive on its buzz,
at last I'm alive, I need its rush
and you must know it's never this
exciting on the paving.
Grand Theft Auto results in a nice long secure stay
at one of those high-walled government 'resortos'.
At night I lie awake
and listen out for the sound stolen tyres make.
Just let me get at your steering
so I can slam your family hatch
through its gearing
until I've floored my life out of the estate,
driven your car far away from all that I hate,
until I make it to some
distant woodland clearing
where I apply the match and watch the flames catch.

WHITE VAN DRIVER

Contemplating consciously,
synthesising subconsciously
embracing existentialism
within a labyrinth of structuralism—
Move it for God's sake!

Travelling with élan and creativity,
the chess master making the moves,
criss-crossing the elasticity of civilisation—
Hey darling want a lift?

A quest for purpose, truths and beyond,
up and down the by-roads
of this inner evolution of the self,
the last words of the prophet
spoken against the burning barricades—
What do you mean I can't park it here!

A surrounding reality
that is filtered through the laminate,
the world is an explosion
of an all-encompassing unity
shining full-beam headlights into the complexity
of time, chance and effect—
Learn to drive you git!

Change is unreal, it is simply
whatever river you flow with,
swept along by its currents—

Get out of the fast lane you Muppet!

You swim within,
using the strokes of the water you were born into.
Taking in air, gasping for beauty,
trying to keep sight of the love that's there.

WE'D RATHER MAKE A FRIEND THAN A PROFIT

This car will get you there and back,
one previous owner, a bloke called Mad Max.
That's not rust, it's surface corrosion
on a scale similar to the earth's coverage by ocean.
I'm only selling it
because I bought it for my son —
and then I realised I haven't got one.
This car will get you there,
only one previous owner a bloke called Ben Hur.
That MOT's a fake?
Now surely that's a matter for a legal expert.
The exhaust is blowing…
but so are the answers in the wind.
The nodding dog just keeps on going.
Make sure you always carry a number for next of kin.
This car will run and run,
one previous owner, a bloke called Homer Simpson.
So the tyres have no tread
but some things are best left unsaid.
The mileage is pretty low —
similar to that of a Boeing 747
that's never missed a show.
Go on give the furry dice a throw!
This car is a good invest,
one previous owner, a bloke called George Best.
Getting the thing to start
is a triumph of luck married to art.
That feeling of being run into the ground
merely means international
car thieves won't be calling round.
You'll never own a better set of wheels —
but the body, the engine and chassis
are subject to ongoing legal appeals.

ON REFLECTION

Your reflection follows you
from the cradle to the grave,
from beginning to end.
It is in one sense your worst enemy
and your best friend.
It is your sole life-long companion.
A mirror, when held to the lips,
shows when your last breath
takes its final curtain.
Nothing is for certain,
because when you stand between
two mirrors
you see yourself reflected into infinity,
for an even clearer picture
enter into a correspondence
with a greater, all-knowing divinity.
Very early in our lives
we learn to recognise
ourselves in reflective surfaces —
the glass doors of the nurseries.
At this point we look at ourselves,
start to ask 'why'
and begin to divide the world into terms of
'we', 'you', and 'I'.
Mirrors have always been there from the start,
the newly forming Earth played its part,
giving us natural dark glass
melted from its volcanic heart.
When we look into each other's eyes
we see the mirrors of our lives.

For a mirror to work it needs light,
that fluctuating ever-present miracle
which imposes a speed limit on the universe
—hold tight.
We walk in that light
with a sense of ourselves.
Our life's own reflection,
staring into our mirrored self
in all its beauty and imperfection.

SKIMMING STONES

The infinity of childhood
is a brief one
full of racing moments,
each vying to be a memory.
Sandcastles built from disposable coffee cups,
a fragile kingdom
created at speed,
slowed by turning pages in picture books,
rapidly layered over time,
measured with string.
cluttered by necessity,
re-charged by car journey sleep,
tidied under duress,
put away in an attic,
rediscovered with awe.

DUSTED

Snow is nature's theatrical miracle.
No man-made design
has the same ambition as a single flake.
No warhead can transform the cityscape,
as snow
gently amassing,
dusting crystallised glamour to the landscape,
sweeping away
the grime and tawdriness of the everyday.
Real life is simply erased,
Its beauty and mystery rephrased,
magically reassembled—
and all this happens
without a single leaf
being trembled.

IN PRAISE OF PRAISE

At school
a child might get
twenty threats a day.
That's around one hundred threats a week.
Which makes approximately
one thousand threats a term.
Three terms a year
brings it up to the three thousand mark.
Over ten years at school
equals about ten thousand threats.
No wonder then,
when asked about their time at school,
so many people reply—
threatening.

MY MATE DARREN

When I was a kid, my best mate Darren
had a great way of getting his toy soldiers to have a war.
He'd line them up on the kitchen floor,
close the kitchen door, draw the kitchen window blind,
set an alarm clock to ring in one minute's time,
switch off the kitchen light, making the kitchen dark as night.
Then he'd take his tennis racquet
and swing it from left to right with all his might,
knocking his soldiers everywhere,
sending them flying through the air.
Making them spin– even his dog joined in,
scampering about with a mouthful of toy soldiers sticking out.
Then, when the alarm clock would ring, whichever side
had the most soldiers still standing would win.
Years later, Darren, now a man, strong and big,
was helping his mum bring in a brand new fridge.
When he moved the old one
he found underneath, in the dirt and the grease,
three toy soldiers who were still fighting the war,
waiting for an enemy that wasn't there anymore.
He dusted them down, stood them gently on the ground
and with as much love as he could,
he told them,
"It's over, you no longer need to be a toy soldier.
You can go back to your wives,
your families and friends you used to know,
lead your former lives. The fighting finished 10 years ago."
As gently as he could he told them "There is no more war."
But no one told his dog,
who ran back in and chewed them up once more.

SMALL VICTORIES

My father's happiest moment
seemed to be watching Prince Charles
being given a brand new, state of the art,
top of the range, James Bond,
five-litre convertible
Aston Martin sports car
for his birthday.
To be totally precise,
the exact moment of my father's
state of euphoria, was seeing
this car break down
100 metres into the Prince's inaugural test drive.
"Look at that, look at that!" screamed my dad,
leaping from his seat
punching the air
and adding, for good measure,
"In your gob, you nob!"
as Charlie, red-faced,
in front of the cameras of the world,
feebly mumbled something like,
"It seems that it'll only start once."
A month later,
the front seat of our Ford Sierra
collapsed under the vast weight of my father
as he got in.
"Look at that, look at that!" I thought,
as I sat in the back.
swinging my knees to safety
like a synchronised swimmer.
I imagine that if he'd been sat next to me,
Prince Charles would have added,
"In one's face, Norman Lyalls."

FIRST WINTER WITHOUT MY FATHER

Each and every week and day
of the winter,
me and my mother knew you were gone
because each and every
hour and minute
of that winter,
we had the central heating full on.

the waterways series is an imprint of flipped eye publishing, a small publisher dedicated to publishing powerful new voices in affordable volumes. Founded in 2001, we have won awards and international recognition through our focus on publishing fiction and poetry that is clear and true, rather than exhibitionist.

If you would like more information about flipped eye publishing, please join our mailing list online at **www.flippedeye.net**.

Lightning Source UK Ltd.
Milton Keynes UK
UKOW05f0607180714

235348UK00003B/22/P